Printed in the United States of America

First Printing, 2017

Educational Partners International, LLC

105 Whitson Avenue, Swannanoa, NC 28778

LAUNCH YOUR CLASSROOM!

BUILDING A FOUNDATION FOR LEARNING

ANTHONY SCANNELLA
SHARON MCCARTHY

CONTRIBUTORS

Executive Editor - Andrés V. Martín

Developmental Editor - Johnny M. Penley

Copyeditor - Shannon Roberts

Lead Instructional Designer - Ryan Hennessee

Instructional Designer - Kristina Lunsford

Cover Designer - Anna Berger

Book Design and Layout - Andrés V. Martín & Anna Berger

Production Manager - Kimberly Daggerhart

Production Editor - Jessica Boyd

Video Production - Johnny M. Penley

To all the teachers that invited us into their classrooms.

Every child deserves a champion – an adult who will never give up on them, who understands the power of connection and insists that they become the best that they can possibly be.

RITA PIERSON

CONTENT

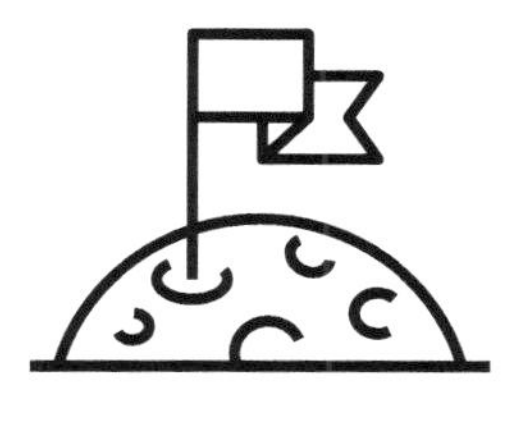

PREFACE

WELCOME TO LAUNCH YOUR CLASSROOM!

About the Book

Launch Your Classroom! is a book for teachers who want to set up their classrooms for success using fast, powerful techniques that maximize student learning. Inside, you'll find some of the most effective ways to begin the school year and build an environment that encourages student growth. We've transformed years of classroom practice and instructional theory into practical advice you can implement now. From learning about your school to building positive relationships with the people you interact with, *Launch Your Classroom!* will help prepare you for some of the most significant challenges in your teaching career.

About the Series

Launch Your Classroom! is a professional development series for educators with a focus on implementation. That is why every professional development book we offer provides a highly visual guide that delivers fast, powerful, and actionable strategies in a way that is easy to understand. Everything we cover is meant to be something that you can use right away. In that spirit, we present you with only the most important information, so you can make the biggest impact possible with the limited time and resources you have.

Every *Launch Your Classroom!* book is focused on finding ways to simplify complicated concepts. We use visuals to help make ideas more concrete and videos to further illustrate key concepts. We provide options for different learning styles!

How to Read This Book

We recommend you start by reading the entire book from front to back. Then, as you continue teaching, you can re-visit sections as you need them. We also suggest that you keep *Launch Your Classroom!* nearby while you're in the classroom, so you can reference parts that relate to the skills you're currently developing.

WHAT ARE ROCKET BOOSTERS?

As you progress through each chapter, you'll notice we communicate a lot of information using infographics and Rocket Boosters. Rocket Boosters are blocks of valuable information throughout the book that provide you with further resources about a topic. We divide Rocket Boosters into five categories:

Activity
Practice and develop your skills!

Highlight
Read quotes, further insights, and advice.

Video
Watch education experts in action.

Reflection
Connect the material to your own teaching.

Complications
Prepare for situations that could go wrong!

Important Note: Rocket Boosters have links to our YouTube channel where you can find *Launch Your Classroom!* video resources. All video resources are also available here:

https://www.YouTube.com/EducationalPartnersInternational

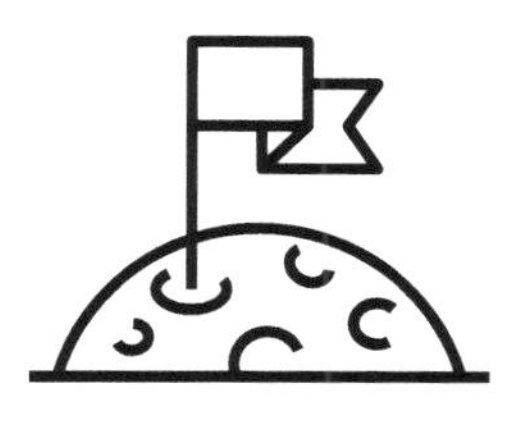

PREPARE FOR LAUNCH

INTRODUCTION

Start Here

Whether you're a veteran or rookie, you're sure to have feelings of both fear and excitement about the first day of school. For many teachers, feeling unprepared can be overwhelming. The first day of school is fast approaching, and if you're not ready, your students will know it.

Teachers who've been in the profession for a couple of years can tell you it's never as bad as you imagine. Typically, the pressure you're putting on yourself is a sign of how much you care about doing a great job. Of course, you already know the value of being as prepared as possible—you did pick up this book, after all!

Often, new teachers face a steep learning curve that can directly impact student achievement. We've spent years working with teachers new to the American K-12 classroom. We've worked with teachers of all subjects across all grade levels. As we developed this book, we observed their transition into their classrooms and identified areas where they could benefit from professional development.
As you progress through this book, each chapter will focus on critical strategies to help you deal with the challenges you're most likely to face.

We'd like to introduce you to Dr. Anthony Scannella and Sharon McCarthy, educational consultants and authors who've devoted their lives to improving educational systems across the United States of America. They believe in a student-first philosophy and understand how critical the teacher is to providing opportunities for learning. They've helped thousands of teachers develop in their professional capacity.

We look forward to working with you as you launch your classroom management this school year, and we hope that you find this book to be an extremely effective resource!

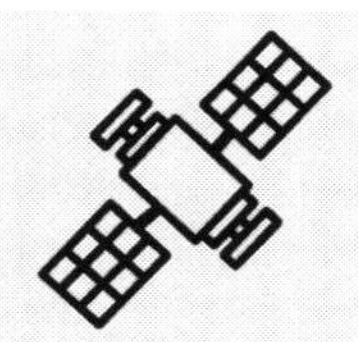

INTRODUCING TONY AND SHARON

Our professional development materials are more than just books. In *Launch Your Classroom!*, you will have access to exclusive video content of your authors and educational experts, Dr. Anthony Scannella and Sharon McCarthy. These videos enhance the material in this book, providing valuable resources, demonstrations, and opportunities for further learning.

To watch this video, please visit:
https://youtu.be/I1H3IWGcD8Y

PART ONE

UNDERSTANDING YOUR SCHOOL AND DISTRICT

PLACE, PEOPLE, AND ADAPTABILITY

Before you start thinking about how you'll design your classroom or greet students on the first day, you need to take the time to learn about your new environment. In the same way you'd prepare yourself for moving to a new community, you need to prepare yourself by learning about your new school and school district.

Understanding any environment comes down to learning about the two P's:

- **Place** - What type of school am I teaching at?
- **People** - Who are the important people to know?

However, when it comes to being successful in any environment, it's always about the big A:

- **Adaptability** - How flexible am I when handling change or managing competing demands?

Adaptability will define your career. It is easy to see the benefit in connecting with the right people and being aware of the school culture, but how you react to challenges will shape your ability to teach. The master teacher is able to stay focused on the goal of student learning, even when new challenges arise.

In this part, we will discuss:

- **Understanding the Different School Types**
- **Examining the Leadership Structure**

In today's world, change is constant. The topics we cover in this chapter will help you connect to your school's human network, which will provide you with the resources you need to adapt to change when the situation requires it.

GO SURFING

If you haven't spent any time researching your school or district online, you should start here. You should definitely visit your school's website, but don't stop there! Schools are a valuable resource in the community, and you should have little problem finding background information and history.

ONE
UNDERSTANDING THE DIFFERENT SCHOOL TYPES

Almost every K-12 school can be described as either a public or private school. The main difference between a public and private school is the source of its funding. Public schools are funded by the government, while private schools receive their funding from anywhere that isn't the government. Who funds the school is vital to understanding how the school operates.

Any organization that funds a school is interested in that school's success. Don't forget, those funds also pay for you to continue teaching at that school. For this reason, it's critical that you always try to contribute to your school's success.

There are different types of public and private schools. In the following infographics, we break down the most prevalent types:

Public Schools

- **Traditional** - This is the most prevalent type of school in the USA. Traditional public schools get their financing from local, state, and federal government funds. Most of the standards they must follow are set by the government. Students attend these schools based on where they live and aren't required to pay tuition. Public school choice programs allow students to attend schools other than the one assigned to the neighborhood they live in.

- **Charter** - Any organization can apply for a charter to open a charter school; however, the state decides whether or not to grant the charter. Charter schools typically receive funding for a limited amount of time. At the end of that time, the state reviews the charter school's performance. If expectations are not met, the charter is not renewed, and the school must be closed. Students must usually submit a separate application to enroll. Often, spaces are limited.

- **Magnet** - Magnet schools are structured similarly to traditional schools, except they specialize in specific areas like the arts, technology, or science. Some magnet schools admit students based on achievement and are generally very competitive. Students typically go through testing and applications before they can attend. Some magnet schools enroll students using a lottery system. Either way, students don't pay tuition.

Private Schools

- **Nonprofit** - Due to the fact that private, nonprofit schools do not receive government funding, these schools do not have to follow the national curriculum. Typically, they are governed by a board of trustees. They usually charge tuition for students to attend and depend on donations or endowments. Examples of private, nonprofit schools' sponsors include religious organizations and private foundations.

- **Parochial** - Don't confuse this with a private nonprofit school created by a religious organization. Parochial schools are directly partnered with a local church that provides the funding. The academic curriculum is supplemented with daily religious instruction. Teachers may be clergy or laypersons. Most of these schools rely on the tuition paid by students. Typically, when expenses go up, so does student tuition.

- **Proprietary** - Proprietary schools are for-profit businesses. Instead of answering to a board of trustees or elected officials, they report to their shareholders and customers, and in this case, the customers are students and their parents. Compared to charter schools that are mission-oriented, these businesses are market-oriented. They have a real responsibility to deliver on efficiency in order to increase profits.

Of course, this is not an exhaustive list of school types. Other types of schools, such as online or Montessori, are beyond the scope of this book.

Next, we'll discuss the important people you need to know in your school!

TWO
EXAMINING THE LEADERSHIP STRUCTURE

Getting to know the leadership structure and the people that comprise it is important, no matter what type of school you're in. For many beginning teachers, the difference between success and failure is not knowing when to partner with school leadership.

Every school type should include teachers, support staff, school leaders, parent committees, and some version of a school improvement team in its organizational structure. Because organizational structures can vary wildly across the different school types, we'll only be covering the most common organizational structure for traditional public schools. If you're teaching at a different type of school, be sure to ask your school leader for your school's leadership organization chart. Let's take a look at the most common leadership structure:

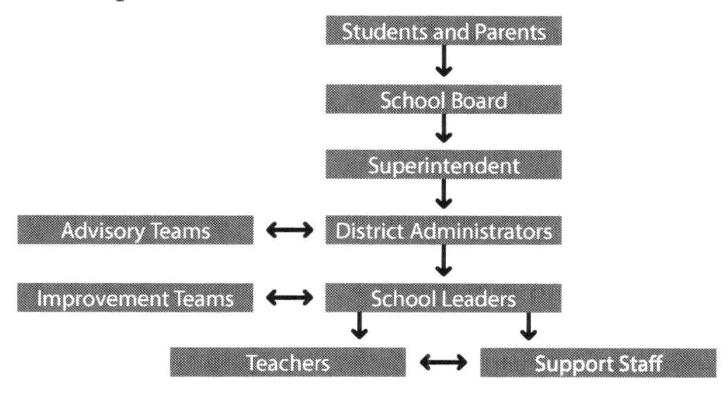

- **Students and Parents:** That's right, we put students and parents at the top of our organization chart. Public schools, just like private schools, eventually answer to the students and parents. After all, they're the chief user of the service you provide. If enough parents are angry or upset about something, you can expect the school board to take quick action to remedy the situation. PTOs, PTAs, and Student Government are formal representations of this body.

- **School Board:** This is the legislative body of the district and exercises control over the educational system primarily through the formation and adoption of policies. Board members are elected by the local community through public elections. Your relationship to the school board is indirect, but you are required to follow the policies they adopt.

- **Superintendent:** This is the executive officer of the school board and the chief administrative officer. They implement the policies adopted by the school board. The superintendent is usually the person who communicates directly with citizens.

- **District Administrators:** These people oversee everything in the district. This includes all physical items (like buses and computers). Typically they also handle human resources, including employee documentation, recruiting, screening, hiring, and assisting with employee termination.

- **School Leaders:** This is usually a principal. You are under the direct supervision of your principal. Administrative policies, communications from the school board, assignments of duty, instruction schedules, and courses of study will all be communicated to you through your principal. You should direct all problems and requests about your work to your principal. You can expect your principal to share disciplinary responsibility and to guide and support you as you work together for the good of the students.

- **District Advisory and School Improvement Teams:** Both of these groups exist to make improvements on either the district or school level. If you are ever asked to participate in one, take it seriously! They're inviting you to add value to your school district, and they expect results.

- **Teachers and School Support Staff:** You should strive to work cooperatively with all school staff members. Make time to see your colleagues. Chances are, if you're experiencing a problem, they are too. By working as a team, you can find solutions faster. If you can befriend a veteran who will help you navigate the school, great! If you can't, try finding another new teacher to partner with.

You should always consider the scope of your request before interacting with any member of the leadership structure. Some questions are better directed at a buddy teacher rather than your boss, especially if you need feedback quickly.

PARTNERING APPROPRIATELY

Eventually, you'll have a problem that's too big for you to handle on your own and you'll most likely need the help of someone within the leadership structure. This is not an excuse for you to absolve yourself of responsibility and turn the problem over to leadership. Just as you have many competing demands on your time, every person in school leadership also has a heavy workload.

Instead, when you need to partner with school leadership to solve a problem, try to present solutions leadership can use in its decision-making process. This way, you convey the message that you're willing to help resolve the situation and not just passing the problem upwards. If you're in the middle of an emergency, you should always follow the established school procedure as closely as possible to maintain safety and provide a good response time. These procedures are created specifically to provide the best possible solution when you don't have time to create alternate solutions.

SCHOOL ORGANIZATION CHART

Find an organization chart for your school. If your school doesn't have one, make one yourself using our chart as a starting point. Once you have a chart, consider:

- Can you match each title to a person in your school system?
- Have you met each person on your organization chart?
- Who should you build a relationship with in order to be successful?
- How are you going to build a relationship with each leader you identified?

CONCLUSION

No matter what type of school you end up teaching at, it's very common to be nervous about starting the school year. If you're anxious, take a moment to remember that everyone within the leadership structure is focused on the success of the school. Since you're a big part of the school, it's in your leaders' interest to see you succeed, too. Schools usually don't bring in teachers and hope they fail!

Take advantage of your new situation and show initiative in meeting people. Say hello in the elevator or cafeteria when it's appropriate to do so. Attend extracurricular activities sponsored by the school. Time is a valuable resource, and in a fast-paced school culture, taking the time to meet your colleagues and develop relationships shows you care. This technique will pay dividends in the end.

Every positive conversation is another step in creating your network of resources. Start off small with the people you work with most often and continue to reach out over time. As you connect with more people, you'll have access to a wide variety of skill sets in your group. This will help you become more adaptable over time.

PART TWO
DESIGNING YOUR CLASSROOM

FACILITATING A LEARNING ENVIRONMENT

To facilitate a safe learning environment for students, a teacher must consider several factors, one of the most important being the classroom itself. This chapter is intended to help you think about the layout of your classroom as well as the necessary supplies you'll need to set up the area. You'll also learn how to set up your classroom with attention to student needs, school and district policy, and availability of resources.

Arranging furniture and decorating your classroom can be a great experience. Although we want to make it inviting and fun, we also need to keep in mind the purpose of the classroom–learning. Every decision you make in that room must be intentional and geared towards that purpose.

The way in which you choose to arrange your desks, organize your class library, or decorate your walls is a form of communication. You're telling your students, parents, and anyone else who may visit that this is how your students will learn this year.

In this part, we will discuss:

- **Taking Stock of What You Need**
- **Designing Desk Layouts**
- **Using Wall Space Effectively**
- **Promoting Safety in the Classroom**

Once you've completed this chapter, you'll know how to gather, use, and store available resources throughout the school year. In addition, you'll learn how to apply some intentional strategies for arranging desks and organizing materials posted on walls in your classroom. Finally, we'll show you how to make your classroom a safer place by highlighting the most common safety concerns and sharing some strategies to limit you and your students' exposure to them. Let's get started!

THREE

TAKING STOCK OF WHAT YOU NEED

You've been assigned a classroom. You're excited for what comes next, but you might be a little worried, too. Don't be! There are some simple things you can do to get your classroom ready.

Meet with an administrator, instructional coach, or mentor teacher. Chances are, your new school has some procedures and guidelines you'll have to follow. They'll most likely be concerned with safety regulations, student movement, etc. You definitely need to follow all of these guidelines.

Also, this is a good time for you to find out what materials the school uses to teach subjects like math, science, etc. Some questions you could ask include:

- Are there textbooks?
- Does every student need one?
- How about math manipulatives or calculators?
- Is there a special science kit or kits that you should have?

All these questions (and other material concerns) should be addressed during this meeting.

Now, the exciting part: it's time to visit your new classroom.

Be prepared for anything—you may find a classroom that's relatively well stocked, or you may find a classroom that looks pretty desolate. Either way, you'll need to take an inventory of what you have.

After you've taken inventory, it's time to submit your request for materials. You may find you need learning materials like textbooks, science kits, or math manipulatives...or your needs might be more extensive, like bookshelves and desks. Either way, your administrator will be able to tell you how to get these items. Most schools will have a procedure for this, so check with your administration before submitting any requests.

In the modern classroom, you'll almost certainly have some level of technology present. From computers to interactive whiteboards, schools will expect you to have some facility with these items. Don't panic if you aren't the most technologically savvy person—you can teach yourself, and the school will likely help with this.

For now, you'll just need to cover the basics:

- Check the technology in your classroom by plugging it in and seeing that it powers on.
- Secure the cords using cord ties, cable covers or other provided items.
- Don't use tape on any electronic cables or devices unless directed to do so by school staff.

After you've set up your classroom, you'll probably find you're still missing some things. Exactly what else you need depends, to some extent, on your own style of teaching.

You might want specialized paper, writing utensils, decorations, etc. The main thing to remember is that most schools will not have an abundant supply of these types of items.

MAKE THE MOST OF WHAT YOU HAVE

School budgets are limited and in some cases, shrinking. It may seem like common sense, but treat your supplies like they're not replaceable. For example: use sheet protectors to cover worksheets students need to fill out. Once they complete their assignment, you can wipe off the sheet protector and re-use the worksheet.

SUPPLY AND DEMAND

When you start to source materials for the school year, it's likely your school will provide you with a materials or supply budget. If you receive such a budget, use it wisely. If you're allowed to space out your purchases over the school year, try to source only materials as you need them (rather than using up your whole budget at once). This will allow you greater flexibility for unforeseen challenges. If you must use your entire budget at the beginning of the school year, try to partner with an experienced teacher for suggestions.

You should always follow your school's policies for sourcing materials. In addition, you should ask your administrators for guidance before pursuing donations from businesses and civic organizations. Many schools rely on contributions like these; however, donations often require special handling by the school. Depending on the community your school is in, parents and guardians can be a final resource for getting materials. Check with administrators before asking parents and guardians.

WHAT'S THE BOTTOM LINE?

When working with a limited budget, it can be difficult to decide which supplies you should ask your students to purchase and which supplies to just do without. Every time you face this decision, ask yourself, "If I take this out, how will it impact academic performance?" As painful as it may be, if it doesn't help your students, you can teach without it.

GATHERING AND STORING CONSUMABLES

Now that you've taken stock of the materials in your new classroom, you'll need to determine what consumables you need. A consumable is any material a student will use and then discard, including pencils, pens, paper, notebooks, tissues, hand sanitizer, and so forth. However you choose to do it, a little forethought about how you'll manage and store your consumable classroom supplies will save you a lot of time and frustration down the road.

Many schools do not supply unlimited amounts of consumables, and you will often need to rely on parents, the PTA, and other sources to obtain them. This will vary between schools and districts, so you'll need to consult your administrators.

You'll also need to assess how much storage the room has. All the consumables in the world won't matter if you don't have anywhere to put them. The same goes for storing student materials. They'll need a safe place to keep their belongings as well as their school supplies.

Check with custodians and office staff to determine if your school has a shared storage area for things like extra textbooks and equipment you won't need for your class. It would also be wise to ask permission to discard or redistribute leftover materials you don't need. If you have access to inexpensive plastic bins or tubs, they can be a great solution for organizing closets or storage spaces.

Check with your school administrators to determine if they have a specific supply checklist. If not, you can find sample checklists for almost any subject by searching online. You may want to check if your school provides any of these items before spending your own money or asking your students to bring them in.

FOUR
DESIGNING DESK LAYOUTS

The room may be set up with desks in basic, even rows when you arrive, but that doesn't mean you should leave it that way. The way you arrange the desks in your classroom will say a lot to your students and administrators. You need to make the most out of your space and use every inch intentionally.

Different learning and teaching styles are conducive to varying arrangements of desks. Here are some of the most common desk arrangements and the teaching styles they correspond with:

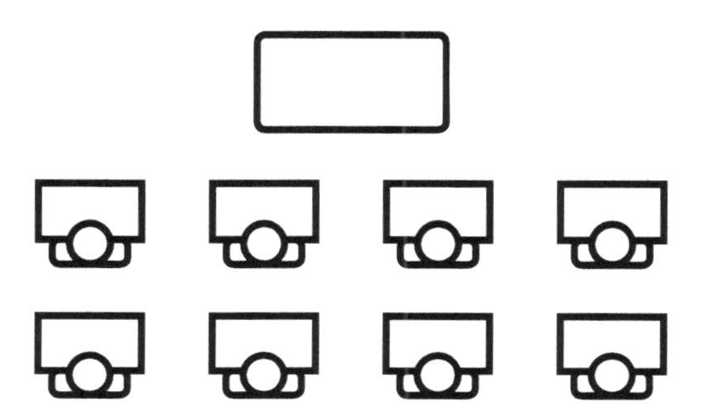

Traditional classrooms usually start off with a standard set of desks in rows. This layout is appropriate for official assessments like testing or any situation that requires each student to have their own private space.

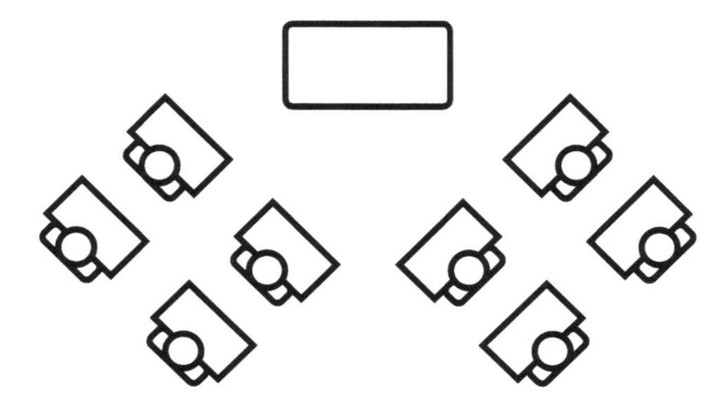

As you can see, the desks in the arrangement above are lined up into columns opposite the teacher's desk or place of instruction. This is a twist on the standard rows that can work well with older students. Each student has individual space, but the columns provide obvious partners and can be easily broken into larger groups when needed.

The desk arrangement above was designed to facilitate collaborative conversation among the whole class. Students in this setup have a clear view of everyone in the class, making it great for discussions, debates, and general discourse.

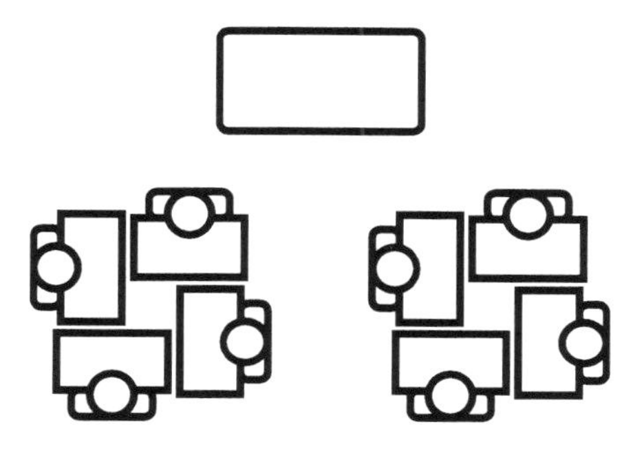

If you plan on having your students do a lot of group work, consider a layout like the one above, where student desks are arranged into clusters for collaboration. While this configuration is mostly used in elementary and middle school, it can still be useful for science and math investigation settings with older students or other collaborative activities.

No matter what grade you're teaching, you'll likely have times during the day when you break your class into groups. You need to provide spaces for the groups to collaborate, whether at their desks, on the floor, or at extra tables in the room.

Make sure the room is organized so that high traffic spaces are clear in case of drills or emergencies. You want to make sure all students can see you, the teacher, at all times, and you want to be able to see all of your students easily.

This brings us to the question of the teacher's desk. The days of the teacher sitting at the desk while students work quietly are over! There will be times where you need to work with individual students, and there will be times when you need to be at the focal point of the room.

Place your desk where you won't be distracted, but also where you can monitor everything that's going on in your room. Keep in mind that the front of the classroom may already be occupied by equipment like interactive white-boards or student meeting space. Do not place the desk near the door - keeping it away from the door will make it harder for students to take things from your desk and quickly walk out.

The way students sit contributes to the way they learn, so don't be afraid to roll up your sleeves, move some desks around, and make sure your room reinforces student learning.

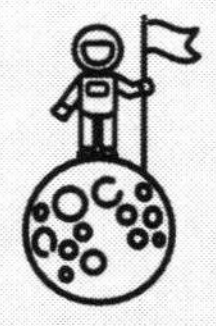

MAP IT OUT

Before you start moving desks, it can be beneficial to make a map of your arrangement. First, measure the size of your room. Next, measure the size of the items you need to fit in your room. On a piece of graph paper, draw your desired layout to scale. For example, one square foot in your classroom could equal one square on the graph paper.

FIVE
USING WALL SPACE EFFECTIVELY

Now that you've gathered your supplies, organized storage, and arranged your desks, it's time to customize the final aspect of your room: the walls themselves!

Classroom wall spaces can be used for much more than simple decoration; they can become learning and activity spaces for students, as well as reference tools. Every inch of the walls should be used with intention. And remember: while it's good to keep things relatively neat and organized, your classroom should always be student-centered. Most of the items you post should be created by the students, and it's okay if it gets a little sloppy at times. Make sure all the images are large enough to see, that any text is legible, and that important items aren't covered up by other postings. Other than that, learn to let go and let the students be in the spotlight.

Don't forget to post all school rules and schedules in a place you can refer to quickly. Leave space on your board to write your learning targets and objectives. Walls should include information relevant to whatever you're teaching at that time, and posters should change and grow with student learning. This is a great way to make student learning evident for parents, principals, and other students who visit your classroom.

Place the posters around the room for students to refer to when working. Your walls can be interactive too, meaning students can mark up or add sticky notes on existing charts. Also: don't be afraid to let students walk up to posters, and be willing to let the wall materials inspire student discourse. Allowing students to interact with and refer to resources that they helped to create will give them a sense of ownership, and they will be more inclined to use the posters to help them with their assignments.

Remember: principals are looking for ways to measure student learning. Displaying student work is a guaranteed way to prove student engagement, involvement, and learning.

ORGANIZE YOUR WALLS

Walls can be designated for specific subjects so students can easily refer to different places in the room when referencing specific content. For example, elementary teachers can benefit from having one wall designated for math; one for science; one for rules, expectations, and procedures, etc.

SIX
PROMOTING SAFETY IN THE CLASSROOM

When you and your students are safe and healthy, students spend more time learning. Also, by promoting safety in the classroom, you'll help protect your school and yourself from lawsuits.

Safety starts with you, so if your classroom is going to have a strong safety culture, you must model safety at all times. If you climb up onto a piece of furniture, your students will assume it's okay to do so, even if you have a rule posted that says otherwise.

Even if no one is injured, when students perceive that their safety is at risk, their ability to learn and perform in the classroom is impacted significantly. If a student comes from a home environment that is physically unsafe, you can expect that student to exhibit negative behaviors while at school. If you suspect that one of your students is a victim of family violence or child abuse, you should follow your school's policies and procedures to report your concerns.

In the following infographic, we provide you with easy solutions for the most common classroom dangers.

EIGHT COMMON WAYS TO MAKE YOUR CLASSROOM SAFER

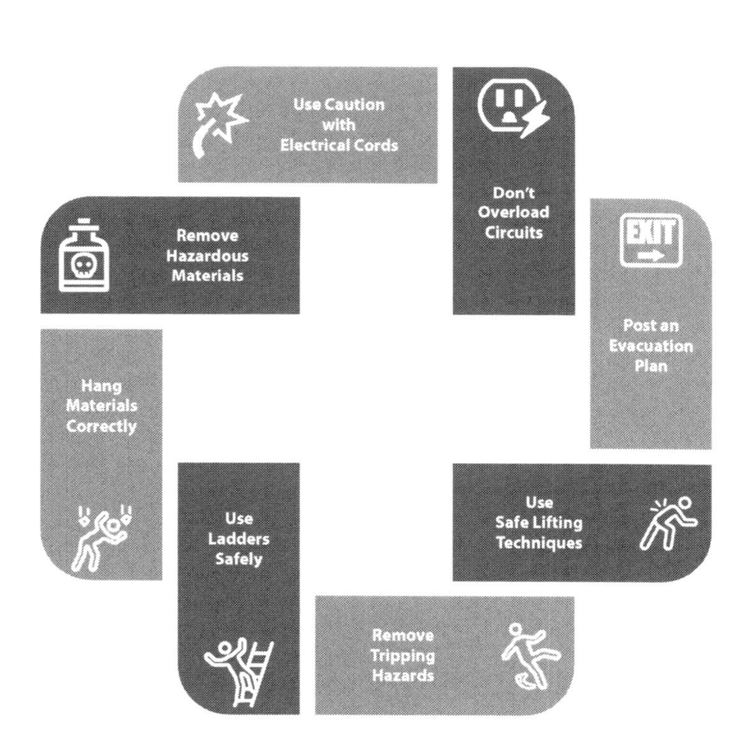

SMALL APPLIANCES, BIG PROBLEMS

Small appliances can pose a severe risk for injury. Items such as portable space heaters, toasters, microwaves, and kettles are infamous for causing scalding or burn injuries. Unless your classroom facility is designed to support a curricular program that involves small appliances, these items should never be used.

CONCLUSION

It can feel daunting to prepare your classroom for the school year, so remember to take a step back and focus on the essentials. As with any big project, your success comes down to making sure you choose the right actions when you need to. By taking time to assess your supplies accurately and following through on sourcing needed materials, you provide the tools for your students to learn. By intentionally arranging your classroom, you provide an engaging environment that's conducive to your students' success. Finally, by promoting classroom safety, you send the message to your students that you care about their well-being.

At this point in your journey, you've taken the necessary steps to create the right physical environment for learning. Next, you will work on establishing the correct emotional environment for your students by developing relationships that keep them motivated.

PART THREE

RELATIONSHIPS FOR LEARNING

THE LEAD CAREGIVER

Every student can succeed—all they require is a caring adult who models positive behaviors. As the teacher, you set the climate for your classroom; you are the lead caregiver. In a successful classroom, students will follow and reciprocate your example.

We all remember classes in which we didn't excel because we felt the teacher was uncaring or uninterested in our success. Likewise, most of us still remember the teachers who pushed us to achieve our potential by fostering a positive relationship with us.

To develop a classroom that fosters positive relationships, you'll need to master these four skills:

- **Creating a Positive and Emotionally Safe Environment**
- **Building Trust and Rapport**
- **Fostering Student Peer Relationships**
- **Using the Keys to Student Motivation**

Good relationships don't just happen. Respect and trust must be modeled, nurtured, and sustained so that positive classroom relationships and the positive behaviors they encourage can flourish.

COMPLIANCE OR COMMITMENT?

This is the core of establishing a learning relationship. A harsh disciplinarian may, after much stress and effort, force their classes into compliance: students following the letter of the rules and meeting only the minimum requirements on assignments.

A teacher that invests in positive relationships; however, is cultivating student commitment. Committed students are motivated by their relationships with their teachers and classmates to perform beyond the minimum and engage with the class.

INTRODUCTION TO RELATIONSHIPS

In this video, Tony speaks about the importance of relationships for learning and shares a story from his own experience about how the lack of relationships contribute to a lack of student engagement and performance.

To watch this video, please visit:
https://youtu.be/mLA_paSM5ao

SEVEN
CREATING A POSITIVE AND EMOTIONALLY SAFE ENVIRONMENT

Well-run classrooms operate on trust. Students will only follow you if they trust that you're invested in their success. Remember that while your position gives you authority, relationships will provide you with influence. A passionate class is a hard-working class.

Before you begin to consider how to foster and manage interpersonal relationships in your classroom, however, you must create an environment that supports and encourages these bonds. In the following infographic, we share our five rules for building a positive classroom environment.

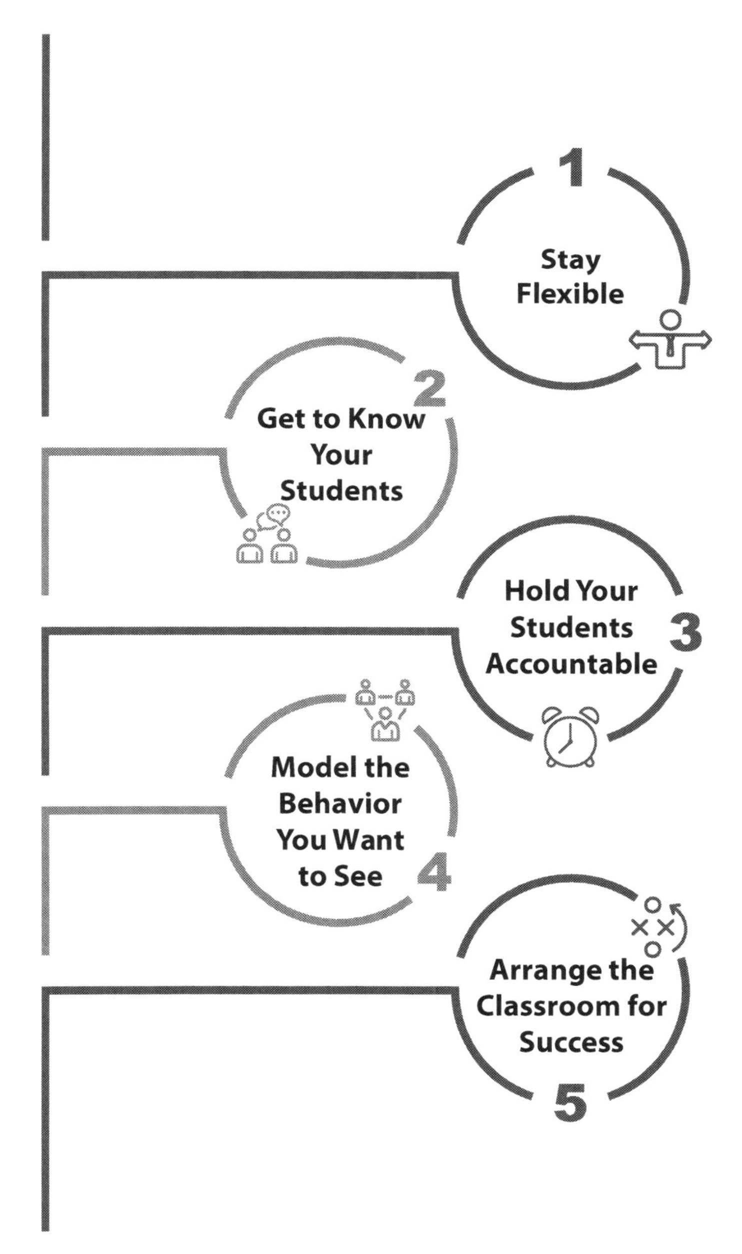
1
Stay Flexible
2
Get to Know Your Students
Hold Your Students Accountable
3
Model the Behavior You Want to See
4
Arrange the Classroom for Success
5

- **Stay flexible:** Planning and prevention are important, but as a classroom manager, you must also remain flexible in the face of challenging circumstances. If something isn't working, don't be afraid to look for alternate solutions. It's important to remember that effective student interventions should work after your first or second attempt.

- **Get to know your students:** Just as developing trust and rapport with your students fosters positive relationships, spending time learning about their personalities and background will help you determine how to manage them effectively in class. A one-size-fits-all policy for classroom management is unfair to some students' circumstances (and is proven to be ineffective).

- **Hold your students accountable:** Accountability is a sign of respect. Expect your students to tell the truth and teach them to be responsible for their own behavior. This will help your students foster self-discipline and increase their productivity. Also, this will provide your students with more opportunities to understand rules and consequences and how they relate directly to their personal actions and behavior.

- **Model the behavior you want to see:** Practice what you preach. If you have a rule that requires students to raise their hands before speaking, raise your own before asking questions. If students must remain silent while walking through hallways, stay quiet with them. Modeling behaviors you expect is key to getting students to understand and support proper behaviors.

- **Arrange the classroom for success:** Don't neglect the classroom itself. Build a class that creates a positive physical and emotional environment. Make the room visually attractive and have supplies and materials readily accessible. Move away from desks in rows and don't be afraid to group your students in different patterns for different assignments. Rearrange your classroom as necessary.

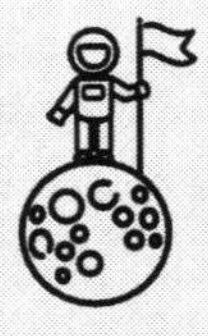

SCENARIO SORT

Below are some examples of strategies or actions that can help you to establish a positive classroom environment. Match each example to one of the rules for building a positive classroom environment:

1. Even though the first couple of times it was a little loud, you continue to move your desks into a circle to accommodate authentic literature discussions.
2. You never go to the restroom during active teaching or work time, unless it's an emergency.
3. Despite being pleasantly surprised at your new routine for morning work, you're still considering adding in a short addition game as a review because students enjoy it and often display a willingness to earn it through their hard work on other, non-preferred tasks.
4. After a student has repeated trouble completing their assigned homework, you intervene. The student says they're just too tired from taking care of their siblings until their working parents come home late. After checking on the student's situation, you decide that they may complete their homework during the morning work time provided for the class.
5. Rather than assigning them silent lunch, you've decided your students who hold side conversations during class should be assigned a journaling exercise

to write about and reflect on the behavior that has caused the consequence.

6. You never stop and chat with other teachers or coworkers when leading your class through the halls.

Answer Key:
1: Arrange the Classroom for Success
2: Model the Behavior You Want to See
3: Stay Flexible
4: Get to Know Your Students
5: Hold Your Students Accountable
6: Model the Behavior You Want to See

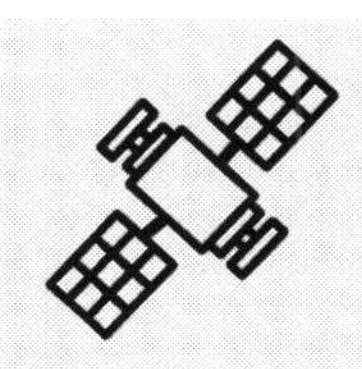

NEVER GIVE UP ON STUDENTS

The art of teaching, of shaping the minds and lives of the next generation, is both incredibly rewarding and exceptionally challenging. You will encounter students that other teachers may have given up on, either due to behavior or performance. Don't ever be one of those teachers. In this video, Tony encourages you to support your students and always hold them accountable.

To watch this video, please visit:
https://youtu.be/DsjSHQctgew

RELATIONSHIPS MATTER!

When we say that everyone remembers a teacher who inspired us to achieve, we do mean everyone. In fact, one of your authors was a bit of a slacker in high school, but an exceptional teacher was able to encourage him to an A+ through fostering a powerful and positive student/teacher relationship. Always remember that relationships are crucial to student success!

BE A TEACHER STUDENTS REMEMBER

With others or by yourself, make a list of teachers you remember – both great ones and inferior ones. Now choose two from each list. See, hear, and feel what it was like to be in their classroom. Identify five behaviors that each teacher modeled that created the positive or negative response and reflect on the following: Do you recognize any negative behaviors from your own practice? Are there positive behaviors that aren't yet part of your teaching style? How can you eliminate the negative and make the positive your own?

FIVE RULES FOR BUILDING AN EMOTIONALLY SAFE CLASSROOM ENVIRONMENT

A positive classroom environment is only half the equation. Students won't fully engage with your lessons or take the mental risks necessary to achieve without a sense of emotional safety. In the following infographic, we discuss our five rules for building an emotionally safe classroom environment.

THE EQUITY DECK

A great way to start building relationships in the classroom is to prove to your students that you're fair and impartial.

Get a regular deck of playing cards and write each student's name on a card. When it's time to call on someone, draw the top card from the deck and select that person. This method ensures that you're being random in selecting students for classroom participation. Once a card is "played," i.e., the student has been called on, the card goes into your "discard" pile and doesn't get reshuffled into the deck until all have been used.

Once you're comfortable using the Equity Deck in your classroom, you can try some fun and effective variations. For example, you could encourage students to think about probability by asking for predictions on who will be called on next, or you could model accountability and participation by putting your own name in the deck.

EIGHT
BUILDING TRUST AND RAPPORT

You cannot build a successful relationship without two elements: trust and rapport. Students need to trust that you're on their side and that your instruction and assignments are designed to help their understanding. With this trust comes a sense of rapport, in which there is a mutual feeling of understanding and effective communication between teacher and student.

On a basic level, trust and rapport are created with students through communication and engagement with their lives. Even steps as simple as learning student names early in the year, greeting students at the door, or finding out about their interests and goals can work toward creating this bond. It's simple, practical, and worth the extra effort.

When students feel a deep sense of rapport with their teacher, not only are they less likely to cause problems in the classroom, often they'll go to the ends of the earth to achieve.

NAMES TO FACES

You can use this activity at any point in the school year to check the strength of your learning relationships, as well as the level of trust and rapport between you and your students.

Make a list of your students in one column, and in the other write something you know about them, such as their hobbies, goals, or interests. Also, close your eyes and repeat the name to yourself. Can you picture the student's face, or are you a bit fuzzy? Make a note of any students you could not immediately picture or recall a detail about. These are the students you need to develop more effective learning relationships with.

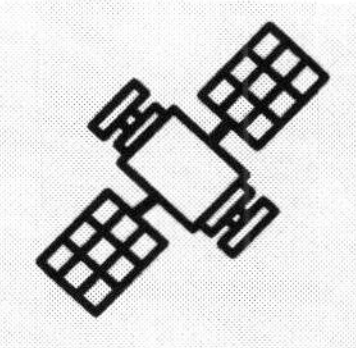

TRUST AND RAPPORT THROUGH MIRRORING

What are trust and rapport, and why are they so critical to forming effective learning relationships with your students, their parents, and your colleagues? In this video, Tony introduces you to these concepts, and how to develop them through the novel technique of physical mirroring.

To watch this video, please visit:
https://youtu.be/GG48mtnPYik

PHYSICAL MIRRORING

If, after spending time getting to know a student, parent, or colleague, you sense that you still don't have rapport, there are other techniques you can try—like physical mirroring. Physical mirroring includes adopting a posture similar to the other person, using similar gestures, and matching the tone and tempo of the other person's speech. The conscious use of physical mirroring greatly enhances a sense of rapport, as the other person will often perceive you as "being like them." Awareness of this phenomenon enables educators to examine relationships and assess the quality of their rapport.

It is important to remember that rapport is a feeling of ease of communication. You can still disagree with a person and maintain rapport with them. Once rapport is established, remember to check and maintain it periodically, just as you would any other element of a relationship.

When employing physical mirroring in your own practice, follow this process and remember that rapport can be achieved while standing up, sitting down, walking, or even on the phone! In the following infographic, we explain each step in the process, then show you how to execute that step.

Mirroring

Matching the body language and speech patterns of another person.

Apply
Sit down with another person and begin a conversation. Observe how that person is sitting and begin mirroring. Make sure to be subtle!

Pacing

Using mirroring techniques at the right speed to synchronize with another person.

Apply
When the other person moves or shifts in the chair, wait about twenty seconds and then move into a similar position in your chair.

Leading

The process of another person mirroring and pacing your body language and speech.

Apply
After about two minutes you may notice the person physically following your moves. This indicates that you can now test for rapport.

Testing

The process of consciously mismatching the other person to check for rapport.

Apply
Test for rapport by abruptly shifting your body or changing your speech pattern. You have rapport if they mirror your change.

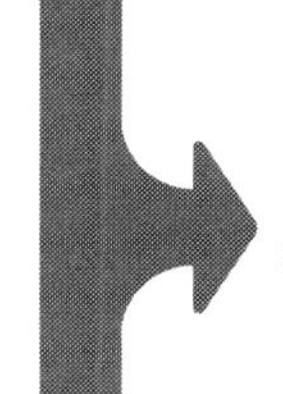

PRACTICE MAKES PERFECT

Practice the physical rapport exercise with three people you know you already have rapport with, such as family or friends. Take notice of when you're in similar physical positions. Try to determine who is leading position changes and make it your goal to be the person leading. If you hear, "Why are you moving every time I do?" this means you need to work on your timing.

POSITIVE RELATIONSHIPS WITH PARENTS

The importance of relationships doesn't end in the classroom. Establishing and maintaining rapport with the parents of students can be just as important. Take advantage of open house events, back-to-school nights, and regularly scheduled conferences—but don't stop there. Contacting parents early in the school year through social media, newsletters, weekly reports sent home with students, and phone calls can make a huge difference in the level of your rapport.

Many teachers create their own websites and use e-mail or other existing online resources from their school to contact parents. However, one of the best ways to establish rapport with parents is one of the most common: the phone call home. Parents are required to be informed whenever their child misbehaves, but an unexpected phone call with good news about their child's achievements can be the catalyst for a long-lasting positive relationship. This technique isn't just effective with parents – many educators say this call home becomes the first choice of students as a reward for good behavior. Below are four different examples of how to get the phone call home started in a positive way.

EXAMPLES OF HOW TO START A CALL

Parent/Guardian

Hello, Mrs. Garrison.
What did Johnny do this time?

Teacher

Actually, Mr. Brown, I was calling to let you know that Johnny came into class this morning ready to learn!

I'd like to work with you and Johnny to engage him further in his learning. Can the three of us meet for a conference?

I'd like to ask you some questions about Johnny's interests in order to engage him further in his learning.

I'd like to invite you to a class activity where we are showcasing Johnny's work.

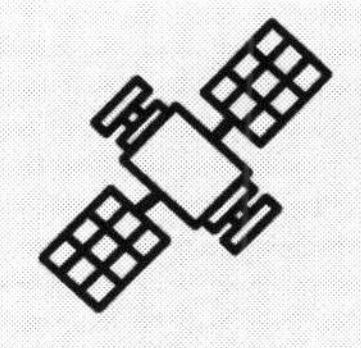

SHARE THE GOOD NEWS

Many novice teachers make the mistake of waiting until something goes wrong in the classroom to contact a parent. In this video, Sharon and Tony demonstrate how to build relationships with parents through a role play scenario.

To watch this video, please visit:
https://youtu.be/fuaXDWkCGQ*0*

NINE

FOSTERING STUDENT PEER RELATIONSHIPS

Finally, the most critical relationship, after teacher-to-student and teacher-to-parent, is student-to-student. Students who develop rapport and understanding among each other contribute to a safe learning environment and are more likely to be enthusiastic and competent in pair and group work.

One way to get students to relate to one another on a deeper level is an Icebreaker Activity. These should be more than simple "getting to know you" activities—they should also incorporate critical thinking skills. Students who think critically are less likely to exhibit negative behaviors in the classroom.

THE 80/20 RULE

To create a classroom filled with effective learning relationships, always follow the 80/20 Rule. During the first two weeks of class, spend 80% of class time on content instruction, and the other 20% on building relationships through activities like icebreakers.

ICEBREAKERS

There are literally thousands of icebreakers out there; however, before choosing and implementing one, evaluate it for critical thinking skills. Here are some of our favorites:

- **Book Title:** Divide students into pairs. One student will then spend two minutes telling the other something interesting or original about themselves. While listening, the other student makes up a book or movie title to capture the essence of their partner. When time is up, have the students change roles and repeat the exercise. Finally, ask for volunteers to share the book title of their partner's life and explain why they chose that title.
- **Self Portrait:** Rather than having students describe themselves through words, ask them to create self-portraits through drawing, collages, craft supplies, or any other visual medium. Keep a stock of old magazines on hand for collages and make sure you have drawing paper and colored pencils or crayons for the artwork. Great craft supplies to make available are toothpicks, pipe cleaners, popsicle sticks, paper clips, glue, and anything else you can find for students to create models. Classrooms equipped with technology can provide an opportunity for students to make multimedia self-portraits such as videos, audio, or graphics.
- **Two Truths and a Lie:** With students grouped in pairs, have them share three things about themselves, with a twist – one of the things is a lie. The other student must guess which is which. Afterward, have pairs report back to the whole group and share their

reasoning behind the guesses they made. After they have made their case, the other student reveals which statement was a lie.

- **Interview:** Group students in pairs and have them interview each other. Instruct them to choose four questions to ask their partner. The interviewer should not ask, "What are four interesting things about you?" This exercise is as much about the interviewer choosing effective questions as it is for the interviewee to reveal interesting things about themselves. Examples could include: "Where did you grow up?", "If you could be an animal, which would you choose?", or "If you could be famous for one thing, what would it be?"
- **Time Capsule:** At the beginning of the year, have students write a paragraph or two about their expectations for the class, what they're most interested in studying, which things they're nervous about learning, and other class-related topics. Afterward, have students share their paragraphs with the whole class. Save the paragraphs. Later on in the year, if a rapport boost is required, pass the time capsules back out and allow students to add another paragraph where they write how they have grown and changed in their expectations, and have them update the class.
- **Mixed Up Attributes:** Break students up into groups of three or four. Have each student write five attributes of characteristics about themselves on separate sheets of paper. For example, "I am a musician. I love animals. Reading is my favorite thing.", etc. Have the group collect all the slips, shuffle them, and lay them out on the floor or a desk. Now the group must work together to determine which attributes belong to which student.

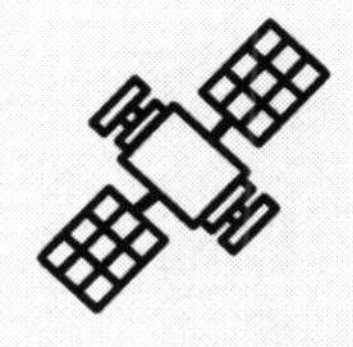

BREAKING DOWN ICEBREAKERS

What would be the title of the book or movie of your life story? Discovering the answer to that question can be a useful and productive icebreaker for you and your students. In this video, Sharon and Tony will explain why icebreaker activities should be in every teacher's toolkit and demonstrate the Book Title icebreaker.

To watch this video, please visit:
https://youtu.be/nVKecrFZgMk

ICEBREAKER PRIORITIZED

Take another look at the list of potential icebreakers in this section. Now, evaluate the critical thinking and relationship skills that each icebreaker encourages. Can you use any of these in your class? If not, can you adapt the icebreaker to fit your subject and grade level? Following the 80/20 rule, purposely schedule your icebreakers and other relationship building activities over the first two weeks of school.

TEN
USING THE KEYS TO STUDENT MOTIVATION

Building powerful learning relationships creates a framework for your classroom, but one aspect is still missing: motivation. Motivation encourages students to act on these relationships and strive for success.

American psychologist David McClelland teaches us that to effectively motivate our students, three things must be present: Power, Affiliation, and Achievement. Power means students have a voice and a choice, Affiliation refers to a student's connections to other people in the classroom and their general sense of belonging, and Achievement represents their feelings of success and recognition.

If students feel these three things aren't present, they will likely be unmotivated. For example, if they feel powerless, they might see their classwork as meaningless; if they feel unaffiliated, their motivation could suffer because they think no one cares about their success.

THE KEYS TO STUDENT MOTIVATION

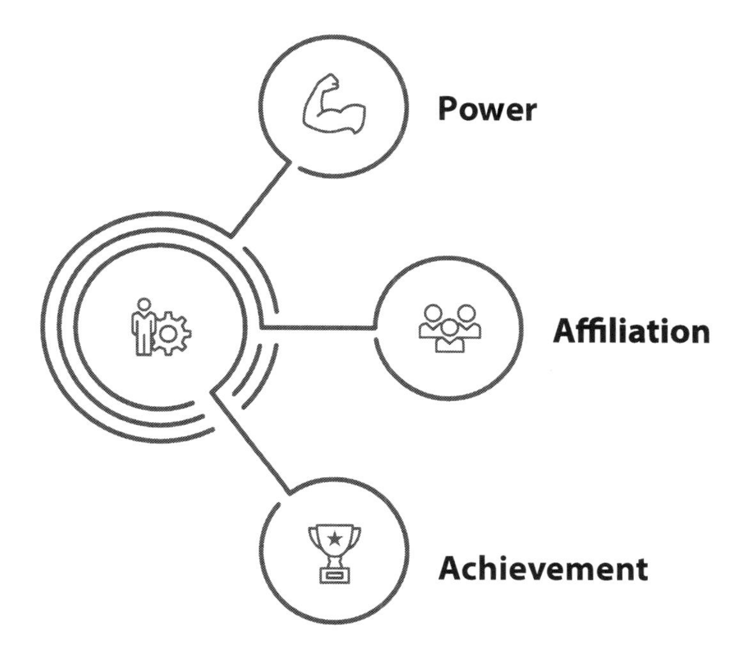

- **Power -** Give students the opportunity to feel a sense of control. Provide choices in their learning!
- **Affiliation -** Help your students connect with each other, the classroom, and the school as a whole.
- **Achievement -** Make sure your students feel successful and, at the very least, make sure they feel appreciated.

UNMOTIVATED STUDENTS ARE LIKELY TO EXHIBIT:

- Feelings of frustration
- Immaturity
- Imitation of negative role models
- Feelings of helplessness or hopelessness
- Classroom violence
- Passive-aggressiveness

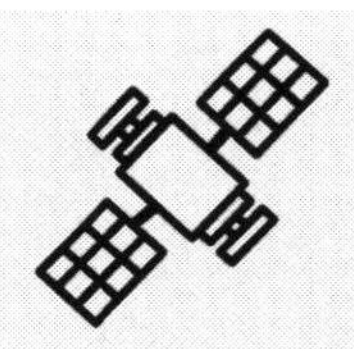

POWER, AFFILIATION, AND ACHIEVEMENT

Why are Power, Affiliation, and Achievement so crucial for motivating students? In this video, Tony answers this question and leads a discussion on ways to develop these keys to motivation. Go through examples of these, and don't forget to listen to your students.

To watch this video, please visit:
https://youtu.be/4rDoqu2gK6E

LEVERAGING POWER, AFFILIATION, AND ACHIEVEMENT

Once you understand why these elements are important, the next step is to determine how to bolster them when certain students are feeling their absence.

To make sure all students feel a sense of Power, try:

- **Learning Goals -** Provide students opportunities for setting their own learning goals, and then track their own progress toward them.
- **Voice -** Consult students on classroom decisions.
- **Options -** When it's time to assign homework, offer up two or three choices and allow students to choose which they will complete.
- **Passion Project -** If a student is passionate about a topic related to the lesson, allow them to approach any assignments from their own interests.

To make sure all students feel a sense of Affiliation, try:

- **Collaboration -** Rather than individual assignments, allow students to sometimes work collaboratively.
- **Mentors -** If both students are comfortable with it, allow one to serve as a peer mentor for a certain topic.

- **Letter Avalanche -** If a student is having a tough time, ask all members of the class to write a quick encouraging note. Bombard them with encouragement!
- **Group Test -** Create an especially challenging test, and then allow students to complete it collaboratively.

To make sure all students feel a sense of Achievement, try:

- **Progress Check -** Provide regular updates to students about how they are progressing through the material.

- **Success Jar -** Have everyone in the class write a recent success they've had on a card. Place the cards into a jar and, throughout the week, take a moment to pull one out and read it to the class.

- **Appreciation Marbles -** Give students a small jar or receptacle and a small supply of marbles or beads. Every time another student does something kind, helpful, or impressive, the student places a marble into their jar.

MOTIVATION RETROSPECTIVE

Take a moment to think about your teaching practice, and ask yourself: What are you already doing to foster Power, Affiliation, and Achievement? Where are the gaps? What new techniques can you introduce to build these motivators? Share your findings with a colleague.

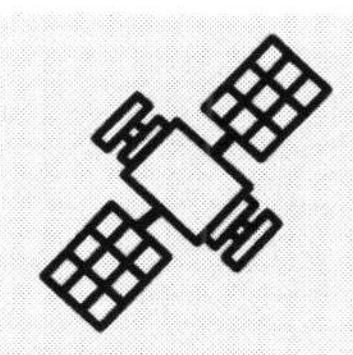

ANYONE CAN GET RAPPORT

Many beginning teachers may feel intimidated when trying to develop rapport with students. In this video, Tony shares a story that emphasizes that anyone can build rapport, even in the most surprising and challenging locations.

To watch this video, please visit:
https://youtu.be/F3TFF5x2Sfc

CONCLUSION

Relationships make a difference in how students perform at school. Setting expectations, establishing rapport with and among your students, recognizing academic and behavioral growth, and making an effort to learn who your students are in and outside of the classroom will demonstrate how much you care. Remember: students don't care how much you know until they know how much you care.

LIFTOFF!

THE EXPERIENCE OF A LIFETIME

Throughout your teaching career, you'll face challenges that test your strength of character. While we've tried to prepare you for the most common problems experienced by new teachers, it's impossible to prepare you for every situation you may face. Instead, we'd like to end this book with our best advice on how to handle any challenge that may come up.

Let's be honest—teaching can be one of the toughest jobs in the world. Often, the work of a teacher can feel overwhelming. Sometimes, it can be hard to even show up for school. If you ever feel this way, please take a moment to slow down and reflect on what you're doing and embrace the reality of the situation.

Nothing worth doing in life is easy. The harder you work at something, the more valuable the reward at the end. Every time you find yourself face to face with a student who makes you feel like giving up, remember to take a moment and think before you act. As a teacher, what you do provides real value. As tough as it can sometimes be, remember what it's all about: the students and their learning.

It's easier to count your troubles than your blessings. However, this type of attitude will only undermine your ability to see the good all around you. For you to stay emotionally healthy, you have to be willing to recognize the good and receive it with gratitude. Negativity is not constructive. We're all learning, and no one gets it right every time.

Success and failure are both parts of the journey of becoming a teacher. In the future, when you reflect back on what you've done in your career, do you expect your story to tell only the good parts? How do you plan to grow if you've never faced a challenge?

Meet these challenges head-on and try your best to be present in the moment. Every potential solution requires you to be part of it. Other people can help you, but no one can ever completely solve a problem for you. Take action by focusing on everything that's working. Leverage the good and never give up on yourself. The moment you give up, you're telling your students and your support network that you're not capable of providing solutions.

Most importantly, when you're facing a problem that seems bigger than what you can handle, remember to focus on making progress instead of seeking perfection. Start each day with the goal of making it better than the last. When you looking back at all the good you've done for your students, you'll know you are having the experience of a lifetime.

We appreciate your reading our book! More importantly, we want to thank you for making a big impact on the futures of our nation's children. Every word you say goes on to influence the lives of our students. By giving your talent, time, and knowledge to education, you're creating a brighter tomorrow. Thank you for inspiring our children to become leaders.

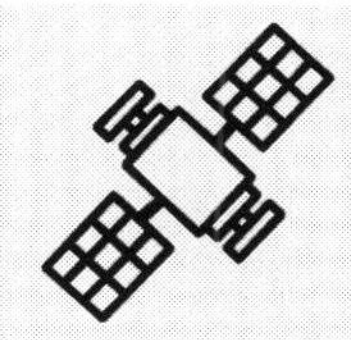

HOW ARE THE CHILDREN

Before you go, Sharon offers one last piece of advice on the importance of student well-being. In this video, she shares a glimpse of a culture focused on the priority of caring for and protecting the young. What would it mean if members of our society greeted each other with a focus on children?

To watch this video, please visit:
https://youtu.be/FQqIBZkeTmQ

ABOUT THE AUTHORS

Dr. Anthony Scannella is the former CEO of the Foundation for Educational Administration, as well as an author, psychotherapist, and trainer in the field of neuropsychology. As the founder of The Principal Center for Educational Administration, Dr. Scannella has worked extensively with school administrators from the United States of America and abroad.

Sharon McCarthy is a national educational consultant and author. As president of Envision, Inc., Sharon works with stakeholders at all levels of the school system and has delivered professional development at the state, national, and international levels.

ALSO FROM EDUCATIONAL PARTNERS INTERNATIONAL

To view all of the videos included in this book, please visit our YouTube page:

https://www.YouTube.com/EducationalPartnersInternational

For additional professional development videos and resources, visit our website:

https://teachwithepi.com/professional-development

NOTES

NOTES

NOTES

NOTES

NOTES

NOTES

NOTES

69681301R00057

Made in the USA
Columbia, SC
16 August 2019